Stone Soup

STONE SOUP

Kate Marshall Flaherty

QUATTRO BOOKS

The publication of *Stone Soup* has been generously supported by the Canada Council for the Arts and the Ontario Arts Council.

 Canada Council Conseil des arts
for the Arts du Canada

 ONTARIO ARTS COUNCIL
CONSEIL DES ARTS DE L'ONTARIO
an Ontario government agency
un organisme du gouvernement de l'Ontario

Author's photograph: John Flaherty
Cover design: Sarah Beaudin
Typography: Diane Mascherin
Editor: Allan Briesmaster

Library and Archives Canada Cataloguing in Publication

Flaherty, Kate Marshall, 1962-, author
        Stone soup / Kate Marshall Flaherty.

Poems.
ISBN 978-1-927443-69-9 (pbk.)

        I. Title.

PS8611.L25S76 2014   C811'.6   C2014-908015-8

Published by Quattro Books Inc.
Toronto
info@quattrobooks.ca
www.quattrobooks.ca

Printed in Canada

This book is dedicated to my parents, Ann and Dick Marshall, who first read stories to me, told our family tales, and inspired me to share my own words.

And to my siblings, Richard and Kristin, who have nourished me with their love and lives.

And to my children, Annie, Gabriel and Locky, who have fed my soul with their generous hearts and astounding gifts.

And to John, my faithful companion, friend and love along the journey.

In memory of Ann Yasuhara and Therese Peets

Contents

DRAGON FRUIT

STONE SOUP

LOST

STELLAR

DISCOVERY

The poor woman could hardly set bounds on her gratitude; and she and the Travelers parted, highly satisfied with each other.

Proud of this discovery, she mentioned it to her neighbors.

By this means the recipe was promulgated;

and it was over the course of many experiments that other pebbles of all kinds proved to make as good a soup as any.

—Robert Moser, 1806

DRAGON FRUIT

Dragon Fruit: The vine-like pitaya-producing cacti of the genus *Hylocereus*, which blooms only at night; the large white fragrant flowers called "moonflower" or "queen of the night"

quaker seat
for ann

wooden bench
like a plain casket
where ego dies

spirit sits
in silence

ponder the space

feel your bones
on plank
surrender
to its support
feet on ground

       meeting-
   house
reverence

 welcome
    simple
        centre

words
not necessary

as silence bathes
both
black and white

holding all
in the Light

here and now

speak
    be heard

listen

Dragon Fruit

You are sitting at a round table
with eleven other guests, slicing gently
into avocado and lime.
There is wine.
Some of you have broken bread.

Music wafts from the outer room, mingled
with smells of roasting yam and maple sugar.

You choose the rustic olive loaf,
tear off a crust, lick your fingers,
their rosemary salt.

On each plate, a slice of something milky-clear.
Dots like poppy seeds or inner kiwi specks.
It must be fruit, but it could be other, almost
of the sea, sushi-like anemone.

Will it be saline or sweet?

A wet drip sticks to your fingertip.
Touch it to your tongue:
sweet water, heavy, a little scent
of something from your Grandma's rose kitchen.

You are told this is Chinese Dragon Fruit, are shown
the green scales with red tips
on the tuberous shape, recalling
a childhood puppet, amaryllis bulb,
the komodo dragon's poison claws,

a little choke of fear in your throat.

Observe the others'
curiosity around the circle—
some slurp it up in sections,
others decline. You imagine
yellow rays of Asian splendour like the sun
penetrating this delicacy.

Only in this era is this possible.
Eating fruit out of season—
you can ingest a patch of light
from another corner of the world.

Shanidar Caves

Stalactite-drip recollections
still sketchy in limestone
images like blood-
streaks on the wall

Outlines
of dark juices seeped
through cracks of rock

Djambe drums resound
deep in stone corridors
and my own heart thrums a rhythm

ja-goon   ja-goon
horse hoof in ancient earth   *ja-goon*
and the throbbing in my ribcage

Whose hands drew horses on these cave walls?

Equine necks slender with spirals
on their ochre flanks
streaks to decorate
their chestnut manes in earth-paints
smeared with fingers
and dotted with pad-tips on rough rock—

horses
jumping over space
in stone

Tao of Night

the moonlit night
or cloud-pocked day

seeds of light in darkness
or bright diamonds on black silk

seeds of dark in lightness
or poppy-seeds on a white bun

which is better?
depends

are you a tailor
or maybe a baker

Hare Krishna Temple

A drop of water in each palm
flower petals
orange garments
bare feet

We chant
        We dance

and pad past the seated one

Wooden elephants
with mahogany trunks guard
while peacocks glitter
teal and sequin-green above him

A monk's brow painted—
yellow lines rise from the spiritual eye
to remind us:
Na ma ste,
I bow to your soul.
(A bit of this light in us all)

Craft in the Woods

Wooden staff in hand, purple cord and tunic,
the caller summons us, "Oyay, Oyay!"
Norse metal rounds his neck,
his voice commanding and gentle.

We follow, tread soft
on grass, form a circle while a priest
cuts the space with a sword.
A witty one sweeps away malice
with a broom. We are spellbound.

The Wiccan priestess, beauty-green, begins.

We turn to each direction—
fire, smoke, water, seeds—
all bow and chant, "Blessed Be,"
Earth's crust beneath our feet, roots,
water and even deeper
rock, space, then fire.

Ponder: we are people
with trunks, limbs, branches, rings of age
who tap the earth and reach to sky.

Standing in the forest,
we too are trees—
different in form but yet the same.

Skinwalker

after Norval Morriseau's painting of a shape-shifter

Forgive me,
I do not know your story,
nor have I walked
a single footfall in your shoes
on the long red road;
I don't have words for "sorry"
in Ojibway.

In sign language, it is the rub
of soft fist on chest, gentle
friction over the heart, like this.
Sorry, I only know your name's
five syllables;
they are famous now,
a mark on the map.

What I do know,
leaning on a cold wall
in a Buckhorn gallery,
is the deeper-than-lichen teal,
rich beaver-pelt brown,
perfect-August-sky blue,
and the slick black
of algae fingers in a river—
I know these colours
in the shapes
you have left for me.

Your painting has gotten under my skin.

I come back to it
after sighting barns
in the gallery
with winter night-lights bright as hay,
sunsets like copper pots,
birch blobs thick as fish soup
with silver scales.

I return to your Skinwalker
on reverent soles.
This painting grounds me—
its clear lines and circles,
yellow-red eye dots,
its colours solid, clear.

I hide under its hide a while,
camp out in awe.
Let us rest here, shape shifter,
pitch our tent together,
my supernatural brother.

Wrapped in animal fur,
what is that split sphere like a ladybug
in your sight?
that stinging point
at your foot?

See, I address now the art's flat face,
not the artist. Norval, ghost-walker,
you have changed yourself
into man-beast-bird-frame.
You have changed me,
for I want to see more
of these three bright eyes.

I come full circle:
Migwetch,
the only word I know.

deified:

reads either way—
left to right
or in reverse—
east or west
towards the holy land
same/same

What does it mean
this word?

magnified
into godly

daily into divine

a reflection

Deus
of non-duality

all
or none
of these
?

Alla
too
(if you release the "h")

inhale *Yah*
exhale *weh*

god
close as breath

in any language

spin the word
on its centre

like a prayer wheel

then

all the colours
mirror
all the colours

Statue

At once I want to place my fingertip
into the scooped-out circles of stone
the size of snow-pocks under an icicled roof.

These drizzled days in January
when the rink turns to grey,
misted air clings
wet just above zero
and blades make soft cuts in ice.

This stone angel is the colour of letdown
after the Christmas star, the colour
of a snowman melting into pavement.

He is looking out over the world,
a little depressed,
his chin in his hand,
his gaze hazy and distant.

I peer into these eyes with centres indented,
glimpse what seems impossible—
eye-curves made of marble,
soft locks of solid stone,
wings feathery but heavy as granite.

What is he thinking in his stone brain?

Of the minotaur of winter?
The insights of the eyeless,
blindness of those with eyes?

The irony of stone wings.

Figure at the Museum of Man

… love is patient and kind

Here
is an Inuit soapstone carving
"Girl with Braid"
standing over an ice hole—
fisher of fish, she is patient and kind,
seeing salmon as through a dim mirror,
the frozen lake.

She baited lines as a child,
ice frosted dull as huffed glass—
but now, her burning heart
thuds under seal fur
in the clashing ice and wind cymbals.

She takes no pleasure
in others' empty nets, but waits
and waits, never boastful.

Each tercet of her braid
marks two years of snow—
three strands woven
for past, present
and future fish-promise —
hope
in each bated breath.

Longing
for the advent of a silver fin
in its perfect time.

Anirnialuk,
God is with us.

Gargoyle/Angel

ii. Angel

From this angle
I see your crooked part,
the burnt tip of your nose,
your slumped shoulders
over scuff-shined shoes.

I glimpse the hollow
in the nape of your neck.

From here
you seem slightly downcast,
lurching toward sunset.

But through the burlap's
cross-hatch weave
I spy that wisp of white mist
that attracts
lightning.

i. Gargoyle

From below
I spy upwards on a slant—
see your scuffed soles,
the worn cork heels,
your ragged panties
and the bottom of your bag.

I see up the slits of your nostrils—
the cross-hatched hairs.

Even from here
on the doorstep
by the grate I feel
the pull in you.

Labyrinth

cool green space—
bright vault above
and light
through cranberry glass

silent sanctuary
of inter-faith paths

four bold corners
hold the maze, not maze,
keyhole map
with candled centre

we in socks
step soft on canvas
and clean footfalls
leave impressions

thinking of what we want
to leave behind

noticing
as we walk side by side
then separate—

the way in is the way out

migrant
for Eli's friend

what disappears after dark
        papers in the rush-to-leave
        through a fence in the night

what lies under the bridge
        clothes, scraps, an orange rind, remnants
        of refuge from rain

what is in the scraps of paper
        a name, birth date, bits
        of story

what was not mentioned
        his marrying a Japanese girl,
        who is pregnant   ten years he worked,
        learned English, went to school, missing
        his family in Albania

 whose are they
        no longer his
        one month to go—
        go back—
        no more words
        no more bridges

who are these nameless
        a population of waiting faces working
        to stay   build
        find refuge
        and after ten years   only a surname
        on a voicemail machine
        to be told one word:
        leave!

Ode to the Roti

Oh Roti—
you are simmerin' curry
squeezin' out just a bit
from your light chapatti wrap.

Oh Roti—
you are so hot, girl,
wrapped in that silvery foil
like one of them carnival dancers
at jump up,
mounds of potato
pushing up at the tinsel.

Oh Roti, your Mama
at Cool Runnings makes you best;
you are the winning partner
in the jerk taste contest—
coupled with Piton, Black Stripe
or Red Cap (with his top popped off)
what a pair you make with ginger Beer—
all smooth, you, and his bubbly grin.

Mmm Mmm …
Roti, you got one fine recipe down, girl,
and you make the band crazy—
Roti, every teenage boy,
after school soccer, wants to bring you home!

Everyone be's nice to each other
when they get a whiff of your
channa and chickpea;
the smell
of your cumin and curry perfume
fills the whole house with a
soft-jaw kind
of sweet anticipation.

Roti, you got to be
everyone's best friend!
(Except Maude, she don't like goat.)

Dig
Children's Site at the Royal Ontario Museum

Locky's hair, still blond as beach,
drips into the huge box.
Goggles arc his brow.

He is lost—
in the grit-sand-shovel-*brush-away*-inspection
of it all; blowing dry earth
from bone, exposing ribbed ridges,
sweeping grit from grooves in vertebrae.

He goes deep,
concentrates with every cell,
crawls over the lip of the sandbox

into ancient sight,
gets right back to bedrock.
and into fossils.

He doesn't read
the "Keep Out" sign,
lost as he is
in history's hairline fissures,
hieroglyphs
and mysterious mounds.

Deep in dirt
and the now,
absorbed in desert dust

he becomes
the dig.

Zatoun

In this pale olive space
we meet,
softer than handshakes,
warmer than the wrap of scarf.

The woman of dark hair and dulcimer strings,
resplendent in a red shawl,
       leans into her instrument—
           santoor sounds like a blessing.

Little finger hammers bounce and sing
      string-music,
           pebbles of rain on pavement.

Her friend with kerchief
holds his drum on a slant,
dayereh drum's
     soft *zanjir* chains
        fall in ripples,
            water-sand sounds.

Sweet almond and nougat cream,
pistachio greens, chai,
a cone mound of sugar—
such abundance—
Iranian sweets and song.

The soft sibilance
     of Persian and poetry
         spilling into spring solstice.

Nawruz, word like a hum,
awakening—
winter greys and hard candy
     dissolving
         making the space
           plush as tassels

on a magic carpet
above the cold March earth.

Peace Pool
at 9/11 site

She sits twisted—
rust, metal, dust—
an iron spine
in a sad spiral.

The day is grey,
wet-heavy;
a bit of mist swirls
around leaden ribs.

This is all that's left
of the twin tower—
bones bent
in a stoop,
an old rag-picker
skeleton.

You have a hunch
as you draw your coat
to your up-shrugged shoulders,
lean through the mist,
to peer at the rusted
wrung-out structure.

You are bundled,
the old lady naked;
you have meat on your frame,
she is mere scaffold;
your flesh, rosy from the wind,
her ribs, picked to the bolts.

I see now
a thread-like spiral,
double helix,
in a wisp of city steam
that rises
from the sewer grate.

White roses pock
the odd engraved name.

We are all made of
these twists of DNA—
the visible
and the not.

The water falls into
an unseen hole.

Apple Slice

You glisten,
little spring blossom grown
to flesh,
like a teenager's Sufi dance
with space at centre.

Your red edge not circle-perfect
but nearly.
Your fine tight skin
shines.

Five-pointed star
within a trinity
of seeds at your core,
you smell
like an angel just left.

Your taste—
not sweet nor bitter—
is not what I expected,
but a slice of reminiscence
grown hard
from a cluster of pink-white petals.

Like a whole galaxy!

I could dip you
in ink and stamp
rough fabrics with your pattern,
regret,

but you are perfect just as you are.

Pyramid Pose

Parsvottanasana in Sanskrit, intense stretch pose,
or making peace with the past—
pyramid, nose-to-knee, and something else I forget.

We all want to be good students, have a sound practice.
Think about it—*Namaste* hands behind your back,
like a reverse prayer, or a forward-looking-

backwards prayer, or an intention
to let go of that past; a leaning
into the now.

Seeing the knee we bend in reverence,
it's a genuflection, but standing.
Try to thank those feet for bringing you here,

oh yes,
and thank that regret behind your back
for whatever it can teach you.

STONE SOUP

Some travellers come to a village, carrying nothing more than an empty cooking pot. Upon their arrival, the villagers are unwilling to share any of their food stores with the hungry travellers. Then the travellers go to a stream and fill the pot with water, drop a large stone in it, and place it over a fire. One of the villagers becomes curious and asks what they are doing. The travellers answer that they are making "stone soup," which tastes wonderful, although it still needs a little bit of garnish to improve the flavour, which they are missing. The villager does not mind parting with a few carrots to help them out, so that gets added to the soup. Another villager walks by, inquiring about the pot, and the travellers again mention their stone soup, which has not reached its full potential yet. The villager hands them a little bit of seasoning to help them out. More and more villagers walk by, each adding another ingredient. Finally, a delicious and nourishing pot of soup is enjoyed by all.

Stone Soup

What a big iron pot
is mothering—cast wide
and heavy as a hippopotamus
smelling of grass and river.

The sound of the spoon like a gong calling
Come for dinner! Get ready! Now!
The kids on scabby knees
scrabbling for paper plates
to pile high with picnic fare,
their mosquito bites tender to the kiss.

Motherhood is an action-word,
connected to the hobbledehoy,
to kinetic energy,
rushing headlong into stillness.

All those stories
of the Old Woman lacing her children
into in a Shoe,
Baba Yaga flying in her butter churn
over a worried parents' cottage,
Dumbo's sweet mother's
trunk in a cradle.

Momo flies across the luminous dusk
in her *djambe* drum,
her body grey from hippo birthings.
She is somewhere in each tale.

Part saint, part witch,
they will string poems of her deeds
into songs at her wake-up funeral,

finding their voices at the stone
as mosses and lichens weep out
words clinging to rock.

In the red tent

we shape stories
and melt beeswax candles
into the nub of night.

Here we sit,
cross-legged on the earth,
leaning back with laughter,
tilting in with listening;
drawing circles in the sand.

The moon cycles her gaze
upon us; we plant
red seeds in secret
and whisper *menses*;
a hush of reverence
swaddles our songs and humming.

We are separate
           for now.

We share our bowls of stew, dates
and wisdom
under the moon's
           soft domination.

We know
there will be sun tomorrow
but for now
           we rest

sacred sisters
in the full womb of night.

When you

open the double doors to
my parents' closet,
the loose mirrors gong
like a singing bowl
announcing the entrance
into cedar smells, plastic veils, and
a confetti of little golden Vs
that once held photos in albums.

A scent of sanitizing, dust,
White Shoulders perfume.

When you look up
to the top shelf,
beside the tiny white dress,
there it is,
the light blue box
with a white dandelion puff!

The "one day" box for
when you become a woman—
white belt, cotton pads with a
thin blue line.

Little red seeds
will crack open soon
and stain ruby on your silk slip—
a gift.

Don't you dare breathe
or puff the dandelion fluff
that will send them
into wings of air.

Close the closet doors,
regard yourself
in the dim mirror
as the light peeps through the crack
for now;
don't let anything in.

Loop

my mother rocks by the fire   hooking a rose green rug   under kerosene glow

she holds her silver J   *poke and pull, repeat,*   the lamp's globe half full

knotted strips at her feet   coarse burlap on her lap   her glasses slip as

rock hook and hum   *rock hook and hum*   she retrieves lost strips

draws them to the light   little woolly heads   pop up in rows and whorls

she does this best   (not hooking but mending)   brings things to the up-side

whenever one of us kids   gets buried   she'll pull us through

mended   forgiven

Teasing

Aunt Mary leans into the mirror
under the dim light
of our bathroom vanity.

She is teasing her hair—
straight up and messy rough—

brushing it backwards, up-
wards 'til it frizzes out
like a kitchen Brillo come undone.

I whisper the secret word:
bouffant!
(the sound as clown-y as her hair looks).

She calls my Mom
Annie-Pannie, even though
she's the younger sister.

Her silver sandals loop through her toes
with a chain; her legs shine
with a Palo Alto tan.

There are sea-gold
strands in her hair.

After all that work
to stand it up, all rough and puffy,
she now pats it back down
and flips the ends up with her fingers
like Mary Tyler Moore.

How does it stay?
That's from the teasing
backwards.

As she smoothes
her California nail polish
over her hive,

I think of after-school,
Rosario and the *mean jeans*
smoking under the bridge,
their tough eyes
on my T-shirt,
and looks that could curl your hair.

Light Within

He seems old now, my Dad,
as he sags into his "poppa chair,"
his taped bifocals slipping down his gaze.

He sits satisfied, after a day of weeding.
His red cardigan has a hole
where mice nibbled one winter,
his T shirt is smeared with goose stains
from basting dinner.
In his lap, a big yellow bowl from the dump.

While the fire sighs down to embers,
and the grandkids wait
for another Baba Yaga story,
Poppa is snapping beans silently
under the golden lamplight.

He twists each stem
like he's trying to be merciful
to the tender greens.

He pinches off the smallest tips.
Nothing is ever wasted;
even these feed the geese.

My pioneer Dad:
bones into broth,
scraps into quilts,
toilet covers into tea cozies.

Every pinch of his green thumb meticulous.
Every word in his stories mesmerizing.
Every scrap of this
made into a useful that;

his careful hands snapping greens
like prayer beads
to feed his family.

Lady Pipes
for Elaine O'Connor

I know
you know that I know—
you guys, during College,
smoked lady pipes
you kept in foil pouches
in your pockets.

You gals patted tobacco,
surreptitiously tamping down
the old boy's club
into bowls you'd smoke,
reading on the sly.

Your lady pipes
smelled richer than Prufrock's haze,

You had *Prince Albert in a Can,*
and let him out!

Mismatched wine glasses at dusk,
leaning out of windows
with blue smoke
haloed round your thoughts,

you were priestesses
of pondering *puff puff,*
possibilities *puff puff,*
and the preposterous question:

why not the moon?

Flight

What matters, then, is that Annie is leaving
for Atlantic shores.
Waves of the ways we'll miss her
mentoring amid mayhem,
the mirth in her eyes.

We are left behind—
the boys and I—
Kings of Siam without their Anna.
The lost boys without their Wendy,
clapping madly because they still
believe in fairies. The magic
when a sister pays attention.

What matters is the shadow she'll leave behind.
She'll not be around to mend the tears,
to stitch things back on, to tell them stories
and remind them, "lovelier thoughts, boys,
and up you'll go!"

They keep the window open.

She will be both here and there,
just like growing up.

A space she leaves for them to step into.

Filth

First it was amusing—
two-year-old you, shrieking
to get that mud-yogurt-finger-paint
off your hands now! Not wanting
the squelch of it, smear on skin,
the primordial slime so close to osmosis.

The other kids in their sandboxes
eating grit sandwiches, rolling on the beach
with coral silt in their cracks,
slopping worms out of soupy puddles,
eating Elmer's glue congealed to lumps like snot
(and those too, who snorted greeners back in).

But not you, potty-trained in a day,
who spoon-fed yourself,
pincher-picked raisins,
spurned brown bananas.

You were a Child of Air—
above the sodden moss and loam—
even your tears dried
without water clay streaks.

Funny how I wish you a landslide,
mud bath, bucket of fermented grapes.

So you could laugh, stomp and slop, just once,
like Lucille Ball stained mulberry
in that Italian vintner's tub,

or that girl who wipes the grimy sweat
off a cross-bearer stumbling in dust.

Mother's Day

It always comes back to bees—
      swarming,
             buzzing,
making astonishing honey out of clover.

I was queen bee on Mother's Day—
humming over
the coloured card
with a jumble of love words
jotted down, a packet
of tissues for tears
and a box of breather strips
for a stuffy nose.
(We laughed
at their fuzzed flannel stripes
stuck all over the headboard.)

I said I'd put them on your father
when he snores—like lazy drones
in a smoked-out hive.

I bet if a bear stuck his head in a hive
that's what it would sound like.

Wonder what we dream about,
with those sounds rasping through the night?
Wonder what the she-bear thinks,
fur-soft, with her cubs in a cave,

dreams over their heads like gauze hats
      keeping in bee-secrets,
            keeping out stings.

Indelible

my first loopy cursive coils—
ooo aaa eee

Grade Four—
under Miss Reed's giraffe lashes,
blinking.

As she stares at my notebook,
her amber pendant dangles.

We are starting cursive writing
                    (what the big kids do)—
Angie loves Warren scrawled on the wall.
Mom writes a list of oranges and soap.
Dad signs a cheque for one hundred and two …

Real ink
spills words in a swirl
onto paper!

No more stubby chubby
thick blue pencils,
and their leaden letters. Now

lilting lovely pen-and-ink.

I stay between the lines
with perfect *ooo*'s that make sense!

Finally a way
for my runaway thoughts
to slip out smoothly.
And stay.

For Mrs. Grunsky

Mrs. Grunsky is stern,
quivers when she plays,
says I am *ready*
for a *real* recorder,
one with a silk bristle brush
to slide down its cherry wood throat,
nestled in a small wooden casket
with velvet depressions
to fit its slim form.

A graduation from the old
brown plastic pipe
with cold holes
and connective squeak.

I love the little pot of resin
like lip gloss for the cork.
(I love this conservatory office.
the place of her practice,
its churchy lead glass windows.)

I place the flat wooden tip
on my lower lip—feel the thirst
of wood for spit—
my tongue suspended
behind a gentle purse.

        I blow softly
as she pencils in
little commas for breath
on the sheet music.

Now I know!
This is
        woodwind
deep as baroque woods
full of thrilling
songbirds.

Moon in Review

i

Sliding the volume bar on a You Tube I copied,
I remember math stencils and the smell
of mimeograph fluid after the teacher
"ran things off" in *dittos.*
That old television on a trolley in the gym
and the entire school watching the scratchy
Apollo landing—
moon rocks, a silver umbrella, an astronaut face
peering through a globe of glass;
riveting, compulsive static.

I recall in black and white—
the chiaroscuro of grainy light and shadow—
that first footprint in moon dirt
stored like fossilized bone in
a glass case. T.V.
"One giant step …"

ii

School was a blur
of lining up, double Dutch,
rote prayers like nursery rhymes
under Sister Enid's singsong on the P.A.,
"Half a pound of treacle … pop goes the weasel!" Amen.
Atoning for the red rubber ball
that made "pockets" against the brick wall:
"You're out!"

The film projectors slapping celluloid circles
when the movie was over.
Paddle to the Sea run forwards and backwards!
The Cree child spitting out berries
and placing them back on the bush;
little Paddle's canoe flipping back up the waterfall
in a reverse cascade of Great Lake froth;
the words on "Rewind" like a foreign dialect
or a lunatic language.

If we could do it all again, we could do it all again.

iii

Our principal forever calling Mr. Di Angelo
to come fix A.V. equipment,
deal with a minor infraction of Snow Rules
or some quibble over appropriate hall-talk.
(When "boobs" was a bad word.)

Not that detentions could mar our enthusiasm—

just look at the new moon!
This place we had visited, planted a flag,
seen ourselves from.
A little planet friend for the Earth,
like Piglet and Pooh,
always so much friendlier with two.
Little sister moon, with her soft-lit face.

No wonder we wanted to befriend her—
our own little jewel in the dream-catcher web
of the galaxy. One in a hundred billion.
Makes us feel not-so-small, despite
all our technology, to know her gaze
is always upon us.

All this mooning
in the space of a two-minute You Tube
I must remember to save.

Born June 6, 2012
for Jannik

... when she opened her heart
in goddess pose
in all those yoga classes,

you were with us
growing in her drum-tight belly,
folding into folds,

twisting into twists,
expanding.
You were that light

within us as we gazed,
accommodating
to your presence,

as she turned on her side for *sivasana*
in foetal position,
resting so sweetly beside your Dad.

You were in the room
each Wednesday night,
most Fridays too, as we

tended to our hearts,
a little bit of us all
in that collective igniting

of air into breath.
Each breath
so much like a tiny birth.

... I am looking for reasons
your life
lasted only hours.

Yet somehow,
in *sivasana*, love
hovers just above reason,

the breath of God hovers
in everything, at times
hidden from sight.

the little things I've learned to love:

the lost eyelash left in the porcelain sink
the sprinkle of raw sugar on kitchen wood
that wing of hair refusing to comply with a lick of spit
forlorn sheet-music scattered
when you know things *off by heart*
plaster fallen from your clay masks
on the mantel next to the angel head
those little marker lines where your thank-you's
spilled over the edges—
the way you *empty the tank* when you run, argue
or prime the piano keys for perfection

those little bits left like chaff
after the combine
the scythe—

fine powder remains
after the threshing

Resentment

hoards in her old house—
cats, scraps, all manner of pots,
the weirdest collection of handbags,
lampshades, jars and pins.

That place on the slant-hill smells
of cat-piss and newsprint. Smells tight, clenched
as a dried-up rosebud.

So much yellowed paper pressed
against the windows you can barely see in,
only the tips of tired book stacks;
the only space in this dank mansion
is the hope of air
through the keyhole.

Lessen 2

What couldn't
please me more,
to be sure,
than less?

What a lesson
is lessening—
I could bless
what is less.

Think of nothing—
then don't stress.
Can you guess?
That is less.

I need to get
fully undressed
(at fifty there's much more
in the less).

My life's so busy,
noisy, and full
of mess,
I need a rest ...

To purge all
that's not best.
Make some space,
empty for the *Yes!*

So much of life
to redress,
to forgive and let go,
I must confess.

I want so much,
and, as such,
need less.

Stone

i
Every boy
should have a stone
in his pocket,
a round piece of rock
to rub with his thumb
when he's scared
he might cry.
Let him rub it smooth
'til sound comes out.

Every boy needs a stone to place
on the rock ledge of remembrance
to keep a place in time
for someone gone, hoped for,
or lost.

Every boy should have a stone
with a sleek surface
like a mother's cheek
or first love's breast,
yet with a sharp nick
to snag the skin
of a fondler's finger—
a tiny v-cut
to remind him
of the call of the crack.

Every boy must have
a stone to skip
across the surface of a lake,
like puberty
lightly touching down
on truth, here and here
and here.

Every boy should have a stone
to suck on
when words have gone dry
or rage has cracked his voice box—
so he can speak again
that sorry sound.

Every boy could
have a stone just to batten
flaps in a storm,
shim a structure,
dam a crack,
flint a light
or tap at a window
where love looks down.

ii
Every boy needs
to swallow
at least one stone,
to feel it lodged in his throat,
that breathless choke,
fish-mouth gape and gasp—
every boy
needs to be silenced just once.
To be a stone.

LOST

Lost synonyms: absent, adrift, at sea, hidden, invisible,
vanished, gone, minus, missed, wandering, wayward,
out the window

Lost

Once I learned the word
migwetch
in a place of sweet grass
and sunlight

I felt many earth-words—
the drumming pound,
Manitoulin sand packed
beneath our feet

a circle of fancy dance
and jingle jumps
rejoicing

recalling how women
were the first drummers
plucking beats
out of needle and hoop
quill, skin

I had a drum teacher once
long ago, we all did
in the womb

fire earth wind
singing like water
timbrel and tongue

cedar boughs on poles
to shade our tender white skin—
gifts we were given
of cloth and craft

the book of strawberry stories
and a ladybug
medicine wheel

the hush of a dropped eagle feather

Re-Entry

Red-eyed jet lag
and a parched throat

it feels as if I've been crying
all night
or drinking gin

but I blink and blink
as I've done neither
yet

flying home from Banff
on a dull silver wing
I watch the sun
rise maraschino

I notice the tiny lines
and rivets on the metal
slide of a droplet
down the porthole
looking out over a sea of peachy clouds

the yellow rheum of city sighs
visible as we descend
ears popping

I don't care for
Sprite or peanuts
the crinkle of snack wrappers
and passenger banter over the engine boom
jarring after months
of Cascade Mountain breeze
and Rundle Summit silence

somewhere beyond
this is your captain speaking
I buckle up and brace for re-entry
as we slide into a summer haze
of smog warnings and cement

the CN Tower points its slick needle's
sharp contrast to rounded mountains
I wince and readjust my vision
and think of the Bow River

valley of your body
I left behind

Magnetawan

Half and half—this astounding split seems odd
from my perch on the pine island.

One side of the sky blue and mid-day bright,
the other a tumble of dark and mutinous clouds

gathering yin and yang momentum—
the bright side with one seed of wispy black,
the ominous side purpling with a point of sun.

Heavy weather pushes in, pudding-thick.
And settles in my belly.

I love the gathering roll of plum clouds,
the electric air, the rise
of wind hackling the hairs on my neck.

The excited birds cling to branches too.
Peeper frogs float still as lily pads.
The loons go under and stay.

The wind whips up, clouds slide in.
Waves of finger-paint darken the page.

Weather's bruise pressed on my sternum
leaving a soft depression
streaked with rain.

Mi-go, Bear Man
Abominable

Someone mentioned the Yeti
in a poem. In my mind I see a Sasquatch,
sure-footed, shaggy as yak, traversing—

something moves in me, and is lost.
What remains, like a footfall in snow,
crystallized in cold, despite

Everest clouds, a peak's pointed finger,
frozen bones of an explorer,
a dung fire at base camp.

What lingers is the shadow,
that sliding shadow on white snow,
the question of

a presence, a promise.
There is such a beast, man, being,
who belongs

on the crust above crevasses,
ice-crisped steeples, the vast white plain—
no stranger here—only to us.

earth

   kicked up
a jawbone today

a few teeth
jut yellow from
the dirt-
ground-tar in its fissures

   long, equine,
the hinge and shape
speak

of one once strong, sleek
with solid hooves
and slender legs

   a once-stallion
now diminished
to mere mandible
bone—

   harness-bit grooves
from pulling
    flattened stumps
from grinding

   now as the rain
begins to wash
this bone

nobility
   slithers
      through its bite

   in tar-sand mud
bits of story
cling to bone

aliens

imagine the centrifuge
of a crop circle—
little cowlicks
of wheat's sun-tassels,
spikelet's spiralling into centre
like snail-shell circlings
or curling proboscis

swirl your mind
from the edges of the field
into lessening orbits—
to one point
at dead-centre

then peel off the outer shell—
dead-centre's dot—
look at its inner core (perfect
germ-speck of gold)

peer into that seed
glimpse the pin of light
(think sand in a pearl,
glint in the eye,
star in a galaxy)

then split that pin into
seven times seven colours,
ROYGBIV,
press your ear
into violet
and hear lavender's
lament—

beyond silence
in the seventh wave—

listen

to what the wheat already knows

mosquitoes

        are so fine
and light—
legs like hairs,
needle-nose a thin pin

wings you can't even see
(although you know they fly)

could be
Pandora's furies
let out of their silver box

minute sound waves
humming in the dark

food for bats and birds
(even their names sound like *Tapas*)

        how your cousins delighted
when m-bugs sparked
in the neon zappers
(and so did you)

        i guess kids like us
loved the sound
of revenge
for a red lump
after the sting

An
  Inchworm
    Reveals
            itself
                 spiralling down
on its silken filament
           twisting gracefully
in the air

this is good medicine

a small green creature
suspended in a prism
of after-rain colourwash

an inchworm
is a caterpillar
that will remain a never-moth
          and wing-less

he doesn't care
          suspended, as he is—
like a breath held in awe
          a puff of relief
                  or candle-bright wish

for an inchworm,
dangling is not a penance

he trusts air,
              believes
this thin thread will hold him

he has become the S-curve
in the centre of the yin/yang—

substantial
despite his tiny-ness,
his dark speck eye
                 winking
weightless
as stilled wind

bovine poem

your liquid eyes that reflect the sky

your soft pink nose
still glistening from the lick
of your thick cow tongue

your ear-tag
nose ring
branded hide

all prove to me your tenderness

cowhands sear your flesh
and pierce it
while still you chew your cud—
an edible reflection on patience—
as you mull over sweet grass
(your velvet forehead furrowed)
swishing your tassel-tail
and nosing clover

what makes you kneel before a rain
share your manger with babes
let your milk
be milked for others' offspring?

your crooning stable lowing
soothes the stall

your moo rumbles
up from the earth

Rocking Northland Rails
near Cobalt, September 2012

I lean against the thrumming wall,
motion soothing my spine.
This rumbling rhythm
tracks up my back to my teeth,
is interrupted by a cry:

   "A bear!"

my eyes too soft
to grasp past the blur of pines …

   … where?

My own lumbering mind,
still hibernating in the hum of travel,
crashes through the passing woods …

   … where?

Too late,
we are past now.
The car lurches from the tracks
a suspended instant,
then cracks back down on steel.

Clouds hang low and full-bellied,
a pastel reminder of the rainbow
arc just disappearing.

I recall all the bears I have encountered:
a gumbling grizzly on a Beehive Mountain switchback,
the scrubby stuffed black bear at Manitou Trading Post,
the she-bear who swiped our dog's snout in the sugar bush.

This bear I missed.

And so, love,
like all those others you wished I had,
this becomes the poem
I didn't write

on the train
that is no more.

STELLAR

Stellar: Related Words:
gravitational collapse, association of stars, blue stellar object,
circumstellar cluster, globular cluster, interstellar light-year,
open cluster, stellar association

Stellar

for Allan Briesmaster on his 60th Birthday

Summer solstice in Pomona Park:
    he pauses,
        takes a breath,

dips down
    among buttercups loaded
with spittlebug spittle.   He sprinkles
    commas, those
gentle gasps,
    creating tiny curved twigs
        on which wings
                can alight.

And like the planets
    brighting around the sun,
      gravity draws others
        to his kind orbits …
          shaper of words   supporter
        of tiny star-specks,
      he connects
     the dots, gathers
    bodies of energy—
 voices and vectors,
elliptical lights.

And spaces too   let
silence fill the
              winter traces carved
in pale snow-shadows;

he can pare down the low-jutting stalks
in snowy sheets of words,
trim the winter fat,
polish up a chunk of ice
until it is perfect.

Next of Kin

Moghur the Neanderthal medicine man
throws powder into the fire.
A burst of blue flame
reveals a tunnel of smoke; he sees far:

Chimpanzees share stick ladders
so ants can ascend to their tongues,
one chimp waves a stick through the air,
conducting a jungle symphony.

A gorilla coddles a kitten to her breast:
Cocoa puckers her lips softly
as if mouthing words.
Somewhere a soft dark ape palm
rests in a bone-yard of ashtrays and tusks.

Washo the chimp has been taught sign language,
has learned to press his thumb
on his upper lip to make the *M* sound—
mama, me, mine.

Mukwa

I am mother
Mukwa
she-bear
bearing my quiver-lip teeth
I splinter the trees
if you get between me
and my cubs

Beware
my thunder
that pops jack pine cones
right off their scraggly branches

When I claw the air
dusty earth
trembles

My licks
slide sweet as honey
over my cubs' ears
and I am soft-pawed
scooping up silvery fish

Odayin, love,
swarms our summers like bees

Yet I can surprise you with my charge
of raw meat-muscle
if you threaten
to harm my cubs

I am awoken hibernator,
queen of the mountain,
grizzly tree-climber
and I can smash you,
send you to earth
like a felled log—

Heed my
swarm warning!
Even my mate-man
can't rip the bark off rage
the way I can—

When I am
barred from my young,
I am
Misabe, Grizzly
she-bear
roaring a warning
so fierce
scree scrambles down the slope

When I awoke

my pillow was soggy,
I had a cramp in my calf.

When I awoke
I had a memory
of someone sending my son
away on a huge ship—
with grey decks, rows of portholes
and waving hands.

He was shouting
but his voice was drowned
by the foghorn's deep whale bellow.

When I awoke
I was waking in my dream,
dreaming of waking up, but not yet.
It did not seem odd
that there was a tattered sheet
for a window, the colour of cobwebs
and cinder blocks.
I lay still in a four-poster bed
by a dresser covered with untouched dust.

When I awoke from this dream-waking—
when I really woke up—
I was sobbing and soaked with sweat,
salty, tousled, and longing
for my son like the sea.

Maus

for Art Spiegelman

I really just got the book
for my teen son, who needs
to read more for pleasure, as
he's lost his confidence
in reading

and so I thought I'd get him
this graphic novel about mice,
one particular Maus,
in Nazi Germany

he says he's "savouring" the book,
reading only a few pages a night
trying to digest
etched images
and haunting possibilities
one tiny bite at a time

I read it in three nights,
had dreams about mice—
cats catching bits
of hidden tails,
false fronts, oven smells,
stripes and starvation's ribs,
enduring silence

hoarding things,
never wasting a drop—
fear of showers,
          and saving, saving, always
saving for a future

this story got under my skin

those little scratchy
pen-and-ink mice
in cross-hatchings and shadows,
        the presence of the past
in scribbles—

left in every corner
of my space, like
mouse droppings—

tiny traps
set to catch my compassion
and hold it,
squeezing me 'til
I couldn't breathe …

my love for this little mouse
deepening
with every frame

words and scribbles
burst free from the book's borders
spilling onto my flannel sheets
like bits of cereal
scuttling sleep

every storyboard cell
a little grist
in the mill of my mind

so i became
a waking dream,
little eulogy,

a love poem
for Maus

To a Russian Fairytale

Dear story,
you pressed a little locket
into my keepsake—
under curved glass
the image
of a gloved hand, goblet,
stream-in-rock, fierce falcon,
feathers.

Oh that devoted bird!
with talons
that tore no Royal flesh as she
alighted each day
on his master's shoulders,
flying in arcs of air
always coming back. Thanks, dear story,
for that constant returning.

That thirsty Prince,
needing always to quench!
You used such thirsty words,
my dear story,
like *silver chalice, sun-parched,
determined, dry as salt.*

Oh the shock
of that royal gasp
when, after a long wait in the sun
to fill his silver cup with a trickle
from the tiny crevice,
the faithful falcon dashed the chalice
from the prince's hand
so the cool water spilled into earth.
Not once, twice, but thrice!

(I loved the way
you did things in threes, gracious story,
and that old-fashioned word for three times.)

By now it was clear the guy was
short on royal patience, eh story?
the way
you made
his lines
so short
and choppy.
Fierce.
How you shocked me
with that royal oath
in squiggly print:
by zounds!
(I tried to say it again at supper,
but Mom was not amused.)

Oh story, what a shame
the fourth and final time
when the falcon was only trying
to save his master from poison.
(You made me wait three pages
for it.) Our loyal falcon
dashed
against the rocks
by his own prince's hand.
Nothing now
but blood and feathers.

The look on that prince's face
when he clambers up the rock,
all sweaty
and grimed with his beloved bird's blood
to see a viper's poison spilled
at the stream's source.

How did you come up with that ending,
my dearest Tale,
to teach us a lesson, surprise us,
steer us clear
of thirsty princes in power,
make us cry for a faithful falcon …

Or was it really true?

A Mouse's Prayer

O constant moon,
you illuminate my tracks,
almost imperceptible
atop this thin blanket
of ice-crusted snow.

May you hide my scribblings
and nibbles
in shadowy corners,
and reveal for my shiny eyes
pearls of hard corn, crumbs
and paper boxes of flakes
I can gnaw holiness into.

Send a beam slantwise
into the farm window,
dresser drawer's raggy nest
of tattered flannel
where my babes lie opaque
in woolen scraps;
where my warm lima beans
nestle together dreaming
six-small-parts-into-one
big mouse dream
of nut butters
and flecks of sharp cheddar.

I will scurry my prayer
across the stone mantel
beneath the clock:

My blessings on all cracks
        and cubbyholes,
my thanks for all things small
        and with seeds,
my wish for protection
        from owl eyes and traps,
and things with lids.

O moon, you see me
        when others do not,
you know my brown fur's sheen,
        and you reflect for me
my own great smallness
in your immensely
        dark and speckled sky.

Rain
for GJF

    made the cardboard soggy
and blue paint has soaked through
    to mush on the pavement.

    My son has packed
all my mementos into this box—
  artwork, cards, favoured toys,
    paper scraps pulped into soft drizzle.

I wonder
    what he is trying to say.

He is lightning-bright,
striking out
to clear away clutter—
fury of *feng shui*
and flashes of clarity—
he has his own designs about
what is no longer needed:
cords stay coiled
in the basement,
the controllers
and scanner stayed,

    but my princess dolls,
  three kings and camel,
tiny boat and music box
    all washed up on the curb

soon snapped up by strangers
  leaving puddles
    of what was
  gone.

I wonder what he was thinking

my angel Gabriel
    teaching me
      to let go.

Sunset

I remember it was dusk;
my child sticky against my breast
as we bumped up and down
the scruffy mountain road

I remember the open flatbed trucks
filled with banana workers laughing
as they bounded down the mountain
after a day of picking

I remember the grey-mauve sky,
the warm and fecund wind on my face,
the brilliant greens of banana leaves
upturned before the salt breeze

I recall the smell of charcoal, grind of diesel,
the thrill of this new place
where the steep curl of cliff
hugged the wheel edge,

the tin-roof shantytowns in scraggy rock
became makeshift bars with nailed-on signs
"*Piton* and *Red Stripe* beer"
dotting the mountainside below

and women by the roadside
carrying raffia baskets on their heads,
hips swaying to the setting sun,
in bright kerchiefs and flip flops

I remember the flash of green—
a neon parrot-lime
just before darkness
wrapped us all

SShh,

we stand before
the image of a grainy Ghandi-ji

(in old sepia
flecked with specks)
slowly placing a finger to his lips.

Sshh.
We are silent as salt.
(Ben Kingsley played him in the film.)

We've sighted *Bollywood* dancing
and bangles, seen saffron powder,
bright as sunshine yokes,

sprinkled over children in *Water*,
danced zumba to *Jai-ho*.
We have read *City of Joy*, the *Upanishads*.

We've guessed at questions
for our fave *chai-wallah*
in *Slumdog Millionaire*,

pondered more than this
                              chanting *AUM*.

We have witnessed
our best friend, the breath,
in *sivasana*,

lit a candle for Calcutta's little sisters,
shouted *shanti shanti shanti om!*

And here we stand, before the screen
gazing into the wise spectacles
of the man

who spun meditations into *dhoti*,
marched miles
to mine the sea for salt,

became the change
                    he wanted to see.

DISCOVERY

of the God Particle

I

                    what is this

?
spark of stuff
            miracle source
fragment of light
            glint of truth

when does air
                    become breath
?

(when) does singularity burst
                              and how
the great flaring forth=

everyeveryeverything
                    from no-thing

OMG
! in all things !

II

Discovery

of God's
Particles

                    what?
life
        source
light
        truth

divinebreath
does something
                              and how
everyeveryeverything

OMG!

III
what the hell!?

nothing
in all things
and all things in
OMG

IV

discover
   !
    in
       all
          things
            !

V

   .   the great flaring forth (big bang OMG)   !!!

VI

holy
        nothing
                 matters

VII

...everythingfromnothingandallthingsinno-thing
andohmygraciousgratitiudemyohmy:
A   L   L   E   L   U   I   A !

VIII

Imagine

giving

mass

...   Alleluia:

mass

giving

Imagine

Amen/it is so.

ACKNOWLEDGEMENTS

"A Mouse's Prayer" was filmed for You Tube and Vimeo by *Micro Films* to the music of composer Mark Korven in 2014.

Untethered Journal of Poetry first published "Efficiency" and "Lady Pipes," August 2014.

Winner of the WCDR "Light Within" Poetry Contest, Piquant Press, for "Light Within," 2014.

Saranac Review, New York, SUNY, first published "earth," 2013.

Vallum, vol. 10, "Magic" issue, first published "Wiccan Craft in the Woods," 2013.

Beautiful Women Anthology, Lipstick Press, first published "Indelible," 2013.

Honourable Mention in the William Henry Drummond Poetry Contest, for "Statue," 2012.

Honourable Mention in the William Henry Drummond Poetry Contest, for "mosquitoes" and "Magnetawan," 2011.

Shortlist Finalist for *Malahat Review*'s Long Poem Contest, "Scrimhold of Reve"; contained the poem "When I Awoke," 2011.

Windsor Review *Filth Edition* first published "Filth," 2011.

Saranac Review, New York, SUNY, first published "Next of Kin," 2010.

I would like to thank Allan Briesmaster, for the gift his undying faith in me—his affirmation and support—and for his amazing eagle eyes and insights. I thank also Luciano Iacobelli and Quattro Books, for their support and the honour of being part of the Quattro family.

I thank also Donna Langevin for her gentle and wise edits and suggestions.

Many thanks to my Aunt Jane Marshall, who read and inventively illustrated many of my poems with a wonderful woodcut and many evocative ink sketches.

I am indebted to Sue Reynolds and her inspirational Writers' Sanctuary Workshops, during which many of these poems were born, to the ever-supportive Sanctuarians, and to James Dewar for the theme challenges at the vibrant Hot-Sauced Words Reading Series that were the seeds of some of these poems. A heartfelt thanks also to Pat Schneider and Maureen Buchanan Jones and the amazing, affirming Amherst Writers and Artists' Method that has nurtured so many of these poems. Such wonderful poetic friends!

I am thankful also for J.W. Winland's "Encounter World Religions" summer course that exposed me to the diversity yet common ground of many powerful faith traditions. And thanks as well to my Scarboro Missions Inter-Faith friends, especially Kathy Murtha, Marilyn Grace, Tina Petrova, Rosemary McAdam and Caroline O'Connor.

I appreciate as well my Muse friends who work-shopped many of these poems with clever suggestions: Clara Blackwood, Joel Giroux, Suzanne Bowness, Rob Colman, David Clink, Sandra Kasturi, Valérie Kaelin, Myna Wallin, and Yaqoob Ghaznavi. I am also so glad of the editing insights of my Invisibles workshopping group: Ian Hanna, Jim Lanthier, Bänoo Zan, Janice Tondrow, Susie Wheelehan, Ann Page, and Aron Tager, and last but not least my kind Book Club friends who challenge and connect with words.

I have learned so much as well about yoga, Sanskrit and the deep meaning of poses from my friends at Main Fitness, especially

Charlene, Gudrun, and Karusia And for all I have learned from Antoinette of Yoga Rocks.

Gratitude beyond words to Mark Korven and Koko for the magical music and filming of "A Mouse's Prayer" and the Toronto Children's Peace Theatre for the space.

I am grateful to the Ontario Arts Council's Writers' Reserve Grant for their financial support in helping to write and edit some of the poems that made their way into this collection of poetry.

Finally, I am so grateful to the Light, that shines in all of us and through all of us, connecting us to each other and to God.

Other Quattro Poetry Books